Full Mouth

New Women's Voices Series, No. 156

poems by

Sara Eddy

Finishing Line Press
Georgetown, Kentucky

Full Mouth

New Women's Voices Series, No. 156

for my mother

Copyright © 2020 by Sara Eddy
ISBN 978-1-64662-338-9 First Edition
All rights reserved under International and Pan-American Copyright Conventions. No part of this book may be reproduced in any manner whatsoever without written permission from the publisher, except in the case of brief quotations embodied in critical articles and reviews.

ACKNOWLEDGMENTS

These poems were written with the generous support of a grant from the Louise W. and Edmund J. Kahn Liberal Arts Institute at Smith College in Northampton, Massachusetts.

Several of these poems have appeared or are forthcoming in journals, as follows:

"Peach Jam": *Causeway Lit* fall 2018 Poetry Contest winner
"Oranges," "Stir Fry," and "First Thanksgiving": *Meat for Tea*
"Honeycake": *Gyroscope Review*
"Ede Market Day": Terrapin Press, *The Book of Donuts*
"A Fall": *One Magazine* (Jacar Press)

Publisher: Leah Huete de Maines
Editor: Christen Kincaid
Cover Art: Timothy McDowell
Author Photo: Jermane Stephinger
Cover Design: Elizabeth Maines McCleavy

Order online: www.finishinglinepress.com
also available on amazon.com

Author inquiries and mail orders:
Finishing Line Press
P. O. Box 1626
Georgetown, Kentucky 40324
U. S. A.

Table of Contents

Peach Jam 1
Butterflied 2
Oranges 3
Prep Work 4
Honeycake 5
Ghost 6
Dickinson's Burrito 7
Ede Market Day 8
Truffle Hunting in Umbria 10
Olive Picking on Election Day 11
Oysters 12
A Fall 13
La Voile 14
No. 9 Park 15
Stir Fry 20
First Thanksgiving 21
Strawberry Syrup 22
The Cantaloupe 23
The Day of Our Divorce 24
Caviar 25
Dumpling Daughter 26
Maggie's Birthday 27
Black Coffee 28
Vermont Muffin 29
Black Raspberries 30
Twelve Tone Grapefruit 31
Ample 32
Donut Song 34
The Great Chef Suicides 35
Long-Term Memory 36

Peach Jam

Sometimes after all the work,
after cutting the cling from the stone
and excising the bruises,
after measuring the pectin
and balancing the tart
lemon with a mountain of sugar—
sometimes still something
goes bad. The pectin fails,
the peaches turn brown,
or in the final moment
a jar cracks in the boil
and the sweet peaches
swirl out with broken glass
into the canning water.
The peach jam was always
yours; I did the raspberries
with their bright tiny pips
and the dilly beans pickled
with garlic and cayenne and
frustration. I wish
I could have seen it, then:
the swirl of sweetness
and danger, yellow flash
and sticky waste has
its own beauty, its own
polyphony, even if in the end
we pick out the glass,
scrub out the pot,
and start over.

Butterflied
   for Elsa

How many raw chickens
have I dismantled with my
bare hands, breaking
their brittle bones
to butterfly their wings
and legs, a violation
of species and physiognomy?
I rub the breast with garlic
salt, pepper, Rosemary,
research again how hot the grill,
then I lay it down to rest
on a bed of iron and oil—
and I think of poultry farmers
and feathers, the twist
of the neck, a final screech
and a bright yellow
eye meeting mine
in anger and sorority.

Oranges

I took them for granted, temple,
navel, and blood;
I ate them under the covers
and stained the sheets
with citrus bloom.
The bent-back peel
sprayed musk in my eyes
while eager for every taste
I scraped the white pith
with my last baby teeth.
Sometimes delicately
I would nibble the very edge
of the papery inside curve
and peel back the translucent
inner membrane so that
my tongue would find
the reward of those teardrop
cells, the sweet nesting
caviar of the fruit's best thoughts.
I took it all for granted.
I ate them like candy,
not knowing they are hybrids
of pomelos and mandarins;
that they are named *Citrus Sinensis*
of the family *Rutaceae*,
they reproduce asexually
and birth new varieties
through mutation. In the arrogance
of childhood, I did not see
the ordinary miracle that
my grandmother's trees
produced these full plump
sweet improbable globes
for me to hoard and savor and suck.

Prep Work

My mother was cleaning shrimp—
it must have been for a special occasion;
we had no money, and shrimp were dear—
but no, she was peeling potatoes
no, she was paring an apple, the knife
curving around the sphere.
But no, it was definitely the shrimp,
a sharp knife defining belly and back,
perfect fingernails peeling back
protective armor and pulling with it
the lovely feathery tails.
She was wearing her green
wool cardigan; no, it was summer,
she was in pink pedal-pushers
her hair was reddish-brown no it
was grey, no—white. The kitchen had
not yet been remodeled; it was 1960's
chic and rooster-canisters held flour;
no it had been transformed to
elegant cherry cabinetry,
1980's linoleum. But yes,
yes, her hand slipped, her knife missed its mark,
yes, it followed the curve of muscle
and momentum and then there was blood everywhere,
the knife falling, her good hand grabbing
a towel and wrapping it already red
and bleeding through, and yes she is yelling
for my father but staying calm, making
sure that though I am young and terrified
I will remember her in control,
I will remember her strong, only
always handling things with grace.

Honeycake

My Son, my beautiful boy
how are you this brave
that when every part of you aches
to blockade the door
and crawl into a corner
you instead say *what*
when I knock.
I celebrate you;
I celebrate your strength
and the wisdom
that made you tell me
your mind had gone dark
that you were straying
and you needed me.
I'll throw a party
with balloons and streamers
for the open heart
that helps you explain
to all your friends
that sometimes you just can't
go to a party, talk on the phone,
get out of bed.
I'll bake a cake for you tonight
and drip a sugary glaze
across its bundty mountain shoulders
for your courage and beauty
and I'll bring a piece to your door
I know you won't be able
to get out of bed
I know you won't be able
even to meet my eye
but I will be prouder than any mother
has ever been of a star athlete
or an honor roll king
when you say
thank you, Mama,
and take a mouthful of honeycake.

Ghost

Every week or two she pulls back
the coverlet in the unused bedroom.
That's all, or, that's all I know.
She may also be wandering
in the air and water, standing
against the walls, inhabiting my head,
filling my body with her own—
her shoulders and biceps in mine,
her fingers in my fingers like gloves
kneading this bread
fold—push—turn—fold—push.
Does she leave my fingers
and enter the dough, waking up
with the yeast to new life?
Does she drive to work, shovel
the snow, pick up the kids?
She's tired out from these days with me;
she feels in her dead bones
the ache of menopause and life.
Even the dead need to rest.
I never used to believe
in ghosts, except when I was
scared of them. Now this one
lives with me, shows me who
she is, and it's like I don't care:
the only ghost I want is my father,
but he's not here: he is no doubt
floating on some Bartok quartet
in my mother's ear. So
when I sneak to the guest
bedroom late at night
and lie down nervously,
feeling her body in mine an
alien and young new thing, I know
that there are scarier things than this.

Dickinson's Burrito

This burrito banging
against my hip while I trudge
up the hill from Sweetser Park
where the fountain bubbles
and the kids climb ancient
apple trees, this burrito
that I'm smelling hungry and tired
while I pass the statue of you
and Robert Frost who
you could not have dreamed of,
the promise of this burrito sustains me
when I trip on the sidewalk
in front of your brother's house
avoiding a group of Japanese
tourists eager for a sense of you.
I'm thinking about your sister-in-law
her beautiful gone son
the careful haunting
of their house. I'll eat this burrito
after the formal yellow house
restored to a clarity and perfection
impossible during your time
of horseshit and chamber pots.
I pick up the Wi-Fi from across the street,
the "Hope & Feathers" frame shop,
its window selling tattoo art
inspired by your poems—anatomical
hearts and deathly moths,
foxgloves and zinnias—then I pass
an electrical box with your name
painted on its side, and I wonder
which of these things would be
most astonishing to you,
Emily—burrito, Frost, Wi-Fi,
fame—or would you,
sorceress, be surprised at all?

Ede Market Day
for Rebecca and Marieke

Jetlagged but game,
we bike from your house in Ede
to a busy open-air market where
farmers sell vegetables and cheese—
Edam, Kanterkass, Leyden—
mongers exchanging wedges of Gouda
for exquisite toy money.
Everything is unreal and wonderful:
this is not our world, we have
no stake, no responsibilities,
and I feel as open and dreamy
as the first green day of spring.
A hurdy-gurdy plays, and children
boogie and fall down and get up.
We walk slowly, we try to take it all in,
we want to buy the whole world
and eat it for lunch. Then we find
the true draw, a stout man
with a stainless wonder:
an Oliebollen machine.
He jiggles a funnel
across a lake of boiling oil,
toggling a switch to release globes
of smooth elastic dough,
plopping them into a smelting
proof to form crisp delicate mounds.
The contraption jerks with each drop;
oil spatters; his hands are
pocked with red marks,
the tattoos of his trade.
Standing in a fugue, I track
the Oliebollen as fluttering gears
lift them from the oil to drain,
and the man dusts them with a ploof of sugar,
a galaxy expanding and settling,
and I feel the gut-tug of love, real love—
falling-in-love love, for that machine
for the sweet smell of the Oliebollen
for the friends who brought us

to this perfect moment
for the market and the town of Ede
and the country of Holland
and the whole world contained exactly
in that round perfect pastry.

Truffle Hunting in Umbria

The little dog's name is Nino,
and he is covered in brown spots
and enthusiasm. We follow him
into the forest, watching
his tail as it tells us the tale
of his nose. At first it is still
and his head is up, looking to
his love, his man Ennio, but then
he buries his snout in the leaves,
and the tail begins to beat.
He snuffles through the underbrush
the fluffy leaves, until
everything stops with focus
and he digs like mad,
his delicate paws precise.
When he emerges he looks to Ennio
quiet face and still little body
he releases the fragrant dirty jewel
from his soft mouth into Ennio's hand
and then his nose goes
to his master's pocket of treats.
The truffle is dirt itself, the fruit
and smell of generation,
and this miracle of a dog
knows how to fathom it and how
not to eat it whole. I would gulp it down
I would have no restraint; the
musty masculine filthy real taste
would be all mine, the rough
nutty texture a quick present
to my tongue, my head
swimming in Italy and hunger.

Olive Picking on Election Day

We were stripping olives, heavy
as grapes and history, from silvery branches.
The grower gave us two gestures:
grab a handful of branches
and yank a hand rake through,
as if combing the hair of someone you hate;
or, reach up high with a long rake
and pull down through the leaves,
using the weight of your good strong hips.

There were 15 of us, mostly women,
mostly over 70 and all of us
tired of cruelty and injustice.
We had been talking politics.
Judith began it: she jerked
her rake down in frustration
while cursing the name of a politician
who would happily burn the world.
It was a joke, a sublimation,
but soon it broke out in riot:
we danced in the trees, snapping
our blades through the branches,
malediction on the names of men
who had corrupted a nation.
Grey hair wove a may-pole of rage.

I spelled out a name, inspired
and we flourished, setting
a hex of destruction. The sound
of the olives hitting the ground
was like bones popping,
and after, when we gathered to lunch,
we poured thick oil on bread
like the blood of our enemies.

Oysters

I'm sitting solo in a bar
watching the game over
a stout and a salad
and I'm thinking of oysters.
Not of ordering them—
they make me wretch, now—
but of the first time, when
you and I struggled through
snow to a cold Cape Cod bar.
We were still in love, but already
I was thinking of other seas,
salty and wild. Still,
when the waitress brought
the pearly circle, the lemon
and cocktail sauce points of light
in the midwinter grey, and
she showed me what to do
(lemon-oyster-sauce, slide
the muscle body down
how repellant, how slimy, what
bravery it takes, that first time),
I was focused for a moment,
in it with you, ready for anything;
and so, happy, to sit across
from you and give this my mouth.
The oyster like another tongue
spoke with mine of the ocean itself
making my head swim,
putting my nerves on edge, and
everything in that small bar
was watching with me to see
what I would do in
that ocean, on that day.

A Fall

What muscles did I lose
to atrophy that year I spent
on the couch, while my hair
fell out and my blood
rearranged itself? Because
here, just a couple years later
while climbing down
a stoneway to the river,
carrying my breakfast
and a book, I find
that the strength in my
haunches that once let me
hike and climb and thrust
myself into this life
is not there, and I am falling
and no one is around but
the white tree mushrooms
watching as my bag flies open
and a hundred black raspberries
confetti the air and fall
on the slick yellow leaves.
I'm fine, I say, out loud to myself
and the mushrooms, and
I've still got the croissant,
though the river will get the berries.

La Voile

and suddenly I'm crying
openly in a French Restaurant
on Newbury street
while the waiter delivers
scallops and duck
and the diners around us
try not to look, and look
anyway and think perhaps
we've split or someone has died.
I'm old enough not to care
what they think, but
young enough to feel afraid
that no amount of Magret
a la D'Artagnan or Coquilles
St. Jacques will calm me down.
We're on a dark topic,
a lost friend, a betrayal
my chest is collapsing
I'm gutted, it's so dramatic, and
my friend, you don't know what to do.
But the crisp white napkin
saves my eyes, and you find
the right thing to say, and I begin
to breathe in the solid lasting
glow of this place and of you.
I can feel it all transforming
already, becoming memory.
What power we have,
to decide what is past,
what is present, and taking
control of our mind's eye
to tack or jibe, take time
by the boom and face the wind
or give it our backs.
The restaurant is called *La Voile*,
and I'm learning to sail.

No. 9 Park
for Stephen Porter

1.
Roasted Pumpkin Velouté
pickled summer fruit, chicharron

We've settled in the stately dining room,
warming up with cocktails
after a fall walk along the Common.
The drinks have silly names: Lion's Tale,
La Mule de Guyane, and you lean on
the French, flirting with the waiter
who deftly pivots to confidante.
The drinks are blushy red.
The way it works here is that it's summer
until you're done with gin & tonics,
when suddenly the pumpkins appear
and the Bourbon. The Velouté pours
from a white jug, creamy and
richly orange, the curve of the soup
like a mother's cradling arm.
You tell me about your visit
to the "White Place," in New Mexico:
an impossible leap, from Park Street
to the desert, from the State House dome
to pale rock formations.
The silence, you tell me in the clash
of this dining room, was heavy
the emptiness claustrophobic.
A catch in your voice, you admit
you panicked a little and
hummed a tune for comfort.
What tune was it; I couldn't hear,
but I wonder now what I would hum,
and whether we all have a tune
that will remind us that our hearts
are still in the cages of our chests.

2.
Swordfish au Poivre
thyme brodo, royal trumpet mushroom

You make me tell stories that you already know;
you want to hear about the time I saw
Julia Child outside the Whole Foods in Cambridge,
taller even than me, yet stooped with age—
and I stopped breathing and felt
light-headed with delight and could not speak.
The Swordfish is crusted with black pepper
and cocoa nibs, and you say "nibs? nibs!?"
to make me laugh. Together we tell each other
about Julia in France, her house and husband,
falling in love with food and life. When you stay
in your studio in Paris, you say, you go out
each morning for a demi-baguette
and fruit, and you make them last
from Beethoven to Debussy
while your hands learn the textures
and flavors of the music.

3.
Red Pepper Cavatelli
pheasant sugo, pecorino, basil

To perform a trill on the piano
you pretend to hold a small ball
in your palm, and placing two fingers
on the keys, rock your hand back and forth
rapidly, making the trill emerge from
a gentle undulation of the wrist
and forearm, rather than the fingers themselves.
To form a petite boule from French bread,
you make a soft cage of fingers and thumb
around the ball of dough; coax a sphere
using a planetary rotation, leaving
a pucker beneath, where the ends
unite, unseen. The French call this
the clé, or key, where it all comes together.

4.
Prune-Stuffed Gnocchi
foie gras, almond, vin santo

All through our childhood
your fingernails were
bitten down with anxiety,
a ragged vulnerability
rushing across the keys.
But one summer in Italy,
you sat by an Umbrian pool
beneath apricot trees,
the sweet-tart smell loosening
the stem of your brain,
and you stopped.
I know this story
like I know my own:
no more ragged nails,
no more wild
thoughts, just the sun
on your forehead and
the luscious arc
of an Étude by Liszt.

5.
Roasted Piggeonneau
rillettes, braised fennel, citrus jus

The joke is about the cafe
on the second level of the Tour d'Eiffel:
something about pigeons and crap and
a mistranslation; I laugh, but I haven't
heard it, really—I've gotten lost
in the round full clamor of the diners,
the golden glow through the Park Street windows,
the beautiful women next to us
so obviously in love, ordering
pink champagne and holding hands.
All of Boston seems spell-cast
for warmth and humanity
good food and fine friends.

Your joke is like the sauce around the pigeon
that catalyzes its fullness and texture
50 years we have known each other
my dear friend. Tell the joke again.

6.
Assiette of Colorado Lamb
tomato & hazelnut romesco, magic molly potatoes

Your mother, daughter
of a volatile Italian butcher, once met
me at the back door in her house dress,
wild-eyed, eating a sandwich stuffed
with prosciutto and sausage,
bits of meat hanging from her lips
like the feet of Demeter and Poseidon
dangling from the Titan's mouth.
I was terrified and enthralled,
caught by her Etruscan strength
and enlisted into your family's
substantial earthy humor.

7.
Cheese Course
Harbison, Pasteurized Cow, Greensboro, Vermont
Tomme De Chambrille, Pasteurized Goat, Poitou-charentes, France
Comte Le Fort, Raw Cow, Jura, France
Pardou Ardi Gasna, Raw Sheep, Pyrenees, France

Like breathing mushrooms,
the waiter says, proud
as if the rind
on this soft harbison
were his own skin.
You give him a smile
that would melt all
this cheese to a puddle,
and I laugh at you
and I love knowing you.
It's been quite the year
for mushrooms in the valley

where we grew up:
Hen of the Woods, Boletes,
Bear Lentinus, and Lung Oyster.
Every hike leads past
jewels dripping with spores,
and the glint and flair
cast an earthy spell.

8.
Mousse aux chocolate
caramelized cortland apples, dark caramel sauce

At the start of the meal you motioned
to our waiter, and asked for mousse
instead of carrot cake as our finale;
an old friend had done this for you once—
a French pianist, student of Ravel,
an old-world sophisticate and lodestar
who taught you to carry
the gift of your Italian-English soul
into the fields of Provence, to play
Debussy with control and abandon
even if the cuffs of your trousers
were frayed. We are beyond fortunate,
given uncommon gifts by family
and fate. This is not really our world,
this restaurant; we come from
middle class altitudes and farm stock,
and we are playing at belonging,
like my mother years ago when
she took me to play the Steinways
we couldn't afford at the showroom
across the common from where we now sit.
But we play with confidence,
and we don't care if we don't quite
pull it off, so long as we convince each other.
I watch you charming the waiter,
your handsome face reflecting candlelight
and humor, and I love the grey hair
at your temples: we are still growing up
together in this flaxen and generous world.

Stir Fry

You've done the sous-chefing, roughly
chopping broccoli, onions, delicate
feathery shiitakes, and arranging
a plate of raw beef, slick and
falsely red, pre-cut by some
supermarket butcher so we needn't
face the truth of it. You don't know
all the things I need, though
some feel obvious to me: garlic,
ginger, soy, sesame, a little
peanut butter. But for once
I just tell you, and for once you
help and keep helping.
I brought this stir fry to our marriage,
my umami dowry, and it's strange
to me that you still don't know
how to do it, that it's still my own
gift, my own burden:
really it's just another little secret
I've kept for you, from you,
that you never asked for, and
time after time with my bamboo spoon
I stir in lies with the bloody meat.
It doesn't take long;
it's a simple recipe.
Soon the meat is browned
and the broccoli tender
the rice is done and you set the table,
chopsticks and napkins, milk
for the kids. We sit down
together and we smile and
nothing is ever wrong.

First Thanksgiving

We're still hammering out the agreement,
negotiating the terms of a 20-year-split
and toeing the edge of a chasm
of insecurity and adventure. But you,
you want one last Thanksgiving together,
sitting down around the table
raising a glass to what: aren't all
toasts really about unbreakable
bonds and togetherness and the future?
We do it, though: we gather our children
and listen to their needs, they bring
their girlfriends as buffers against
awkward, and it is fine. It is fine.
You do the cooking, rooting down
in traditions of turkey and potatoes,
asparagus and stuffing—your stuffing
that is one of the best things
of our doomed marriage.
You dig your heels in and vary
hardly at all, despite the weirdness,
despite the newness
of our lives in which we will have
to decide for ourselves whether
turkey is right, or maybe it will be
pheasant or ham or something absurd.
We put a half smile on it, and we enjoy
the hollandaise, and we begin
just barely to think of next year's meals.

Strawberry Syrup

My fingers are dripping red
from hulling these berries,
searching out and excising
the rotten parts that will ruin the jam.
The pile of hulls and rotten berries
rises up in the sink
but I'm persistent; I find
the good stuff.
This is the first jam I've made
in my new life, and I've left
all the equipment behind with you.
I crush the berries with sugar
and pectin, fill the jars
with a jury-rigged funnel,
and boil for 10 minutes.
Then I sit and listen
for the pop of the lids
telling me that it's all ok,
that the seal has taken,
the process is complete.
But the next day
when I turn over the jars
the pectin hasn't gelled
and the jam runs up the sides
a bloody red mess. So
I start over, and add rhubarb,
take my own time with it all.
The sloppy first try
will still taste of new beginnings
when I prise open
the first jar in midwinter
and call it strawberry syrup.

The Cantaloupe

Read through the lace,
the reticulated net, ropy & rough
to see the orange blush beneath;
smell the stem end,
the omphalos of dirt, stalk,
transpiration, xylem,
and generation; push that
navel with your thumb,
thinking of your baby's fontanelle.
This is how you know
it's ripe, and the flesh within
will be bright milky sunset orange
and sweet all over in your mouth.
You would not eat cantaloupe,
not even though you craved it,
for fear it would not be perfect.
The prospect of disappointment
was too harrowing for you,
while I dove in teeth first
to melon after melon,
eating my disappointment
down to the rind, forgiving
the overripe and the ordinary
for the chance at perfect, ripe joy.

The Day of Our Divorce

After the pistacchi cake
drizzled in rose water,
after the Za'atar and sformato
and all the wines—Valancey and Anjou Blanc,
Roberto saying "You're on a roll, Sara!";
after lunch with my gracious mother
who tells me she's proud
and uses my own face
to smile at me;
after the long walk dazed
and unearthed but breathing
new air and feeling the tiny
new buds of spring
and the rush of the river;
after divorce court, the rage
emanating from you like fumes;
after "thank you your honor";
after all that and a day that broke
open to the sun, my headlights
on the dark street surprised
a doe, light-footed and bright-eyed,
who sprang to the side of the road
and then turned her glowing
orange eyes to mine
for a long quiet moment
while the earth began to turn.

Caviar
for cwh

While packing up to leave my house
and my marriage, I find a tin of caviar,
fish playing in a faded green sea
among the Cyrillic letters on the label.
It was a gift from a boy decades ago
when I was barely a woman, new
in my body and luscious with love.
He had been to Russia, and
swam with thoughts of me
when he saw these fish—emblems between us
of love and play. When I packed up from that love,
tucked our letters and our eternal
ephemera in a cardboard box,
I added this tin, and I swore
I would only open it
and put my lips to those salty eggs
when I fell in love again—the young
woman's prescience, that of course
I would do that, I would replace that early
training-wheel love with something
more solidly, austerely adult. And I have.
I've had a whole lifetime since then
of late-night open hearts, mad sex
in pine woods, moon-gazing
woozy-headed love. I had a marriage
that was worth at least ten of its twenty years,
and a love affair worth all the time it took.
They were all exquisite, all wonderful,
loveable men. But here in this box
is this tin and its funny happy fish,
all these decades later, still sealed shut.

Dumpling Daughter, Weston, MA

Glimmery glass noodles slip
and shimmer in the bowl
with chips of beef like continents,
and our conversation ranges wide
from trauma to laughter to food.
You are both tired.
Adulthood is a planet
of weariness and woe, we say,
and even these crescent-moon
dumplings swimming in
sweet-sour-hot can't
make it all better. The mail
won't carry itself, and the books
won't sell themselves, and the
children don't raise themselves.
For a passing space, though,
chopsticks arc from
dumpling dish to pungent sauce
to mouth, and I feel the warmth
in my chest of old friends
and care, and umami comfort.

Maggie's birthday

Maggie was turning 91,
and we had a party for her,
beef stew, celeriac and carrots
in butter, a sensible poppyseed cake;
there were cocktails and wine—
her generation knows how to drink.
When we talked about poetry, she said
oh, well, I've got a story for you.
She said when she was younger—
younger, she said—she and her girlfriend
knew James Wright, they were all
poets and artists and all young and mad.
On the day that JFK was shot
they all gathered, poets and others,
to drink and console. Jim, she said,
got tight, and he gathered her up
like a foundling goat
under one arm, and her fabulous
poet girlfriend under the other,
and he charged through the house
like some great midwestern god.
He was very big and very strong,
she said, the liquor making cartoon
images above her head
of a minotaur poet with two
rascally rabbits beneath his arms.
It's hard to imagine on that day of all days
they would have flared out
with this life, this exuberance
and yet, perhaps this is exactly
what poets do—get tight
and carry each other
as protest, as weapons
of defiance against despair.

Black Coffee
   for David Porter

In the quiet back room
we stood at the window
feeling the warmth of our cups.
I let the bitter fruit
of the coffee inform my gut
that one day I might have something
smart to say. I had come to him,
the elder scholar, New England
formality and kindness,
for life advice, and he brought me
black coffee from his kitchen.
I felt formal and old and sanctioned.
He had just mowed the back yard.
The grass was crisp.
But there were clumps of bluets,
here and there, delicate fairy flowers
that toddlers pick for their mothers.
He saw me notice. *Eleven*, he said:
he had mown perfect circles
around eleven patches of blue,
marking their beauty,
their passing importance,
dancing with a lawnmower
to preserve the play of summer.

Vermont Muffin

Into the trash it goes,
dry and stale and simple-sweet,
the complex promise of its dark
chocolate crown unfulfilled.
It looked so perfect and personal
in the glass-front case
next to cider doughnuts and fudge,
but the sign out front says
"big game reporting station"
and they don't mean Harvard v. Yale,
and the box of shells next to the muffin case
has neither whelk nor razor clam.
I'm deep New England but an outsider here;
the counter girl pity-smiles
when I point to it—I'm a liberal rube
from Massachusetts, I don't
know any better, and I've never
shot a gun or held the head
of a bleeding bear. They should be
only good, muffins: one tender foot
in breakfast, the other in dessert.
This one should have been a reward
for a rainy walk through this bleak town
feeling disconnected and hungry,
a tourist writing a fake name
and a false origin in the guest book,
imagining myself someone else,
eating a better muffin on a sunny day.

Black Raspberries

Blackberries, big as almonds
and plump with late summer,
have a flat taste that hits the
back-of-the-tongue, hardly sweet,
but plentiful by the pond
when the snapping turtle has
lumbered off to lay her eggs.
They're easy picking. Your
smell, though—I look up
to your eyes swimming
in the sweet surprise of it—
is the delicate, kind
black raspberry. Peppery,
rolling on my lips and the tip
of my tongue. I would stain
my hands reddy-black with you
and take you in by the handful,
I would make jelly of you
on a hot summer day and not mind
the scalding pectin or sugar.
There are so many poems about
blackberries and men; but you
are not like them: there is nothing
easy about you, and this is not
a love poem: you destroy
me and you open me up.

Twelve Tone Grapefruit

There are twelve sections
in every grapefruit, hidden
beneath the thick bitter pith,
and each section holds part
of my body, dismembered
and lovely. Taste it
take it into your round
little belly, your man's
belly, and tell me you
love it. Count it up
1 to 12, play the tones
of the row on your horn:
breasts hips lips,
make a feast of it all,
hold your mouth around it
tell me it is exquisite
the pearly perfection
the sections so sweet.
Paint me in a series of
citrus portraits, bright
with California fire
brush the tang and pop of
every cell of my body
on every canvas. And then
spit it out; go ahead
and tell me it was
never for you. See
if I believe you.

Ample

I've decided to move past
my salad days, my small-
pot-of-yoghurt days,
give my appetite free reign,
and crown myself
Queen of the Gluttons.
Today I will eat 3 bowls
and I'll take an extra plateful.
I'll eat a field of greens,
a pasture of cows,
a coop of chickens.
I'll tip back a crock of kimchi
and gargle it down
with a flagon of rye.
I'll eat an ocean of shrimp;
I'll eat an ocean.
I'll eat the trees on Monadnock
and the mountain itself
my mouth will unhinge
and take in with their joy
all the people in this town
and their dogs and babies,
their sorrow and suffering
I could eat their sins
and their shameful bodies
scrape their hair from my teeth
and pull the roads through my bite
like the leaf of an artichoke.
I'll roll through town with
a sumptuous belly, picking
my teeth with church steeples and
drinking satisfaction as a digestíf.
My body will be glorious
and huge, the rolls of fat
a landscape of desire,
my thighs pillows of pride.
I'll take up room and I'll take
my time; if you say
my body is overmuch,
my physique grotesque,
I will devour your judgment,

and your soft eyes will pop
like caviar between my pearly whites.

Donut Song

What do you do when your favorite donut shop
is shut down, shuttered by the greed
of a predatory landlord
who monstrously dismisses
Boston cream and chocolate frosted
buttermilk and Bavarian cream,
the soft flesh of their cake and yeast
as yielding and tender
as new shoots in spring. Where
will they go, the friendly local baker
and her cast of unlikelies
who served me warm smiles
and coffee and dainties from the oven?
Give me jelly-filled,
old-fashioned, maple-frosted,
give me the delight of the rashly
unhealthy, the lusciously bad,
and give me the strength
to hunt down that landlord
and leave on his doorstep
the cut-rate and stale
mass-produced abominations
of the nationwide chain, for
donuts make the last and best
of our earthly indulgences.

The Great Chef Suicides

We imagine that with the most beautiful food
on earth, and the most delectable companions,
tattooed and elegant, consuming music,
truffles and foix gras, you could want
for nothing, you could be only happy,
simply happy, as if that were something
people can be. We put us into you
and feel shaken and disappointed to find
that in fact you really were just us,
just this ravenous and insatiable,
always ordering the wrong thing
and burning the roast, and starving,
starving for the meal that will give us peace.

Long-term Memory

Human memory splits into short and long, and then long
divides into semantic (facts, dates) and episodic
(stories, events). Semantic is tough: I forget the names
of characters in favorite books, I lose which president
was the worst, what street I lived on in Ann Arbor,
the names of my old students. The stats on Pedro Martinez
when he pitched for the Red Sox are gone, and the different
breeds of horses and clouds. I don't remember chemical formulae
or the measurements for the scones I make every damn week;
how to reset the clock in the car; how to hard boil an egg; how many
minutes per pound for turkey. I don't remember who won best actor.

My mind rolls over and sheds all this usefulness aside, leaving
episodes and dreams, nuance and invention: Pedro Martinez
tells a story about a mango tree, and he is fixed in my head, my
heart, human beyond baseball. Faces and feelings and melodies,
the time we drove out to Walden and you played a "Pond Song"
on your sax. Because I care, I remember bread milk eggs
panko avocado tequila flounder dish-soap lemons
birthdays school events doctor's appointments summer plans,
I remember the kids' first loves, my first loves; how to hold
a rabbit so it's calm, how to mop the floor, how to
make a bed, tie a Windsor knot, cry in public, mow the lawn.

It's not all fun: I remember navigating the dark
back room at the end of my workday, past the stockmen;
a doctor saying "don't tell your boyfriend about this."
I remember every single time a man has said something
uncomfortable. But also a Lucky Charms kiss, tomatoes
warm in the sun, the creak in a friend's voice, an egg
in a San Francisco diner. Long and short, episode
and fact, date and story, I stretch from the day I began
to bleed to the spider scars on my lover's legs;
that remembers me, I said as a little girl, and casting my net
around way back and just now, I remember me.

www.ingramcontent.com/pod-product-compliance
Lightning Source LLC
LaVergne TN
LVHW041554070426
835507LV00011B/1082